The Cottage On Zeus Park

Endearing Tales from a Simpler Life

By Suzanne Briley & Ilse Wolff

Written by: Suzanne Briley & Ilse Wolff
The Cottage on Zeus Park.

LCCN: 2020924019
ISBN -13 : 978-1-5136-6852-9

Design & Layout by Kaylyn McCoy

First Printing. Printed in the United States of America

RECIPE FOR HAPPINESS

Ingredients:

     1 pinch of children or grandchildren, well behaved
     1 medium dog, preferably an adopted mutt
     1 cup full of friends
     1 1/2 boxes of good books
     1 large hammock
     2 or more shade trees
     1 generous bouquet of flowers from the garden
     3 cups of home-grown mixed greens without aphids
     1 bottle of good wine
     1/2 whiff of bread baking in the oven

Combine all ingredients, generously flavor with music,
art and poetry and stir with loving care for a lifetime.

If needed, add a bicycle and kayak for extra zest,
and for decoration sprinkle with a sense of humor.

BON APPETIT

Meet The Authors

By James D Snyder

Suzanne Briley

Phone Suzanne and you never know whether she'll answer "hello" or plunge you into the middle of a running conversation. When I called to tell her I was about to write this foreword, it was Lady Macbeth who answered: "Oh, terrible tragedy! What am I to do for dinner?"

Seems that she'd invited her grandson over and had a quiche cooling on the kitchen table. "I went in the bedroom for only a minute and when I came back it had disappeared." That is, until she looked down to see the quiche plate spattered on the floor and her dog "Batz" licking the last of it.

Mary Poppins would have given the dog his comeuppance. Suzanne decided that Batz might not comprehend his crime. Otherwise, Poppins-Briley could be two peas in a pad, so to speak. In 1996 Suzanne descended upon a cottage in Hobe Sound that needed loving care. In her carpetbag was a patchwork of creative innovations wrapped in ribbons of experience. Raised in an Antebellum home, Suzanne was groomed to be a concert pianist and was the first female to graduate from the Florida Atlantic University music school. After adding acrylics and watercolor to her artistic portfolio, she defied convention in the 1970s by launching an all-woman sportswear manufacturing company in Palm Beach. After crossing the million dollar sales threshold and being featured on national TV, she wrote a lively book about it.*

Financial success opened the way to another new life: summers in the English Cotswolds as a trail-walking nature guide and sponsor of classical concerts under the auspices of Oxford University.

By then Suzanne had a new last name, thanks to Ed Briley, who arrived with her to set up housekeeping in the cottage on Zeus Park. Ed (who left us in 2012) was a fun-loving bon vivant, eager to atone for a misspent past in the staid world of theology. With Suzanne at the piano and husband Ed as a garrulous tenor, the two were often the whole concert at functions in Florida and England. They were also impresarios of practical jokerism, many of which were inspired by trying to top one another.

Into the Zeus Park cottage Suzanne and Ed brought two lifetimes of paintings, pottery, pooches, pranks, teapots, a grand piano and some strong notions of how people ought to squeeze the most out of a day. For a neighborhood they picked a place where homeowners frown furtively on the relentless onslaught of wider highways, monster McMansions and big box chain stores. The Brileys also chose a small town whose founding fathers thought they were "classing up" by naming the circular expanse at the center Zeus Park and the nearby school The Apollo. In between were streets with names like Mars and Olympus.

Since then, Suzanne and neighbors have made what one could call a Herculean effort to maintain their "Old Florida" lifestyle.

* Doing Business in a Palm Beach Taxi, by Suzanne Bonner Briley, 2014.

Ilse Wolff

I first sighted her at a country club tennis gathering in 2012 where this lithe willowy blond was outplaying women and men alike. Surely, I thought, she was somebody's daughter just down here visiting her folks. I learned that she was seventy, recently widowed, and wintered in Tequesta.

Amazing. And Intriguing.

The first delve into Ilse's persona usually begins with her German accent. Despite being born in the most hellish part of World War II, she remembers a "happy" childhood playing among the rubble of bombed-out Berlin "because we didn't know any better." She will always remember not having enough food, and her mother's tearful despair when frost ruined a bag of precious potatoes.

Because Ilse's family lived in the U.S. sector, she learned to appreciate American jazz and generosity. When she became a Pan-Am stewardess "to see the world," 21-year-old Ilse had already learned English as an exchange student in England.

By the 1970s, she was living in New York, raising a daughter on her own after her prince charming turned out to be an abusive husband. Out of adversity came self-reliance: delivering clams to restaurants, running a roadside food stand, securing a frozen yoghurt franchise – always a step up the ladder of life and always too proud to write home for money.

Other skills evolved on the same trajectory: from painting her own furniture and sewing her daughter's dresses to buying a first house, expanding it, then designing and building a larger home – and eventually building her dream home on a pond in Long Island's opulent Southampton.

Art in many forms moved with Ilse on the same upward path. Today stunning charcoal portraits hang in her Long Island home that she drew at age sixteen. She owns five varieties of electric saws, all used when she carves wood, makes stained-glass windows or frames her own paintings. In recent years she has focused on watercolors and the unique framed schools of "Stoned Fish" she arranges from beach shells and pebbles.

If you compare their resumes of careers and travels, Wolff and Briley would seem to share little in common beyond painting and a love of classical music. Rather, the magnetic pull comes from a shared joie de vivre and a puckish sense of humor (such as blurting out something outrageous and staring innocently as the shock waves ricochet around the room). More than anything, both exalt in seeing/doing something *new* – spotting a rare bird, a special sunset, or imaginary sculptures in puffy clouds.

Here's that "something new" in action. Recently we had a failed, fizzled hurricane. I'm sound asleep the next morning. There's a tugging on my arm and Ilse is saying, "Get up. The TV is showing the kite boarders on Juno Beach and I want to go see them."

"Why?" I mumble.
"Because the waves are up and the kite boarders are sailing forty feet in the air!"
"Nice."
"Have you ever seen kite boarders jumping forty feet?"
"No." And so we went to the beach.

By now, you may have discovered that I pursued the lady tennis player from the day I laid eyes on her. We're now life mates, with each day an adventure in something new.

(Disclosure: I was compensated with chocolate chip cookies to write this. JDS)

How This Book Came To Be
By Ilse

The first time I laid eyes on Suzanne was at my annual country club art show. Nothing fancy, mind you, just great art from dabblers and serious artists alike.

The Riverbend Country Club in Tequesta is quite modest compared to others, but it is filled with fun-loving, wonderful people, snobs and phonies not welcomed.

So there we were, sipping cheap champagne, ogling the paintings and nibbling on food everyone had contributed, when all of a sudden this smiling, white-haired lady walked up to the clubhouse piano and started to bang out a boisterous Boogie Woogie! It was foot-stomping fun! Unfortunately I never had a chance to meet her that day and tell her how much I enjoyed the entertainment, because I was busy talking to admirers and potential buyers of my art work.

The next time I saw Suzanne was at one of her house concerts on a Sunday afternoon. A friend of mine had asked me to go and she described these concerts as something quite special, and she was right. About a dozen people had come to this cute cottage to hear music, mingle and enjoy some homemade cookies, as well as little English tea sandwiches with - what class! - the crust cut off.

Sitting down on an eclectic mix of chairs in the quaint, art-filled living room, the concert began, and what a wonderful performance it was, classics and jazz played on piano and guitar. The intimate setting made it very special, and I treasure the memory to this day.

During that afternoon, I found out about "The Barn". I learned that, instead of a garage, Suzanne had a great big barn next to her house, where all kinds of artists met once a week to paint and inspire one another. My ears perked up and I wanted to be part of that group in this intriguing setting and under the auspices of this wonderfully crazy, life-embracing lady named Suzanne. I asked, she graciously said YES, and I became one of the Barn Artists.

To this day I still feel excited at the prospect of going to Suzanne's barn once a week, painting, walking in her lovely garden, having lunch in the gazebo, laughing at her wonderful, quirky sense of humor, and maybe going home with some homegrown kale, basil, a tomato or two, or a cup full of mulberries.

And then one day, out of the blue, Suzanne approached me and asked me if I would be interested in creating a book with her, and how much fun we would have doing it. Just like that! The book would be filled with anecdotes from life in her cottage, with local lore, poetry, recipes and lots of our art and ideas, flavored with a touch of humor.

Hmmm. Coming up with a book at OUR age? After all, we are not even middle-aged anymore, and who would read an actual printed book, written by two little old ladies with crow's feet and unwanted nose and chin hairs?

But I was intrigued, and without thinking about it much longer, I said

"Yes, what a great idea"!

Again: Just like that!

Osprey Cottage
By Suzanne

It all began many years ago when Ed and I moved into a small house, which we named "Osprey Cottage" in honor of those amazing birds. It was a former gardener's cottage, once belonging to an estate on Jupiter Island. It was given to the island's barber, Mr. Letterel, as a gift by Joseph V. Reed, a prominent New York socialite, diplomat in Paris, patron of the theater and developer of the exclusive enclave of Jupiter Island. The small house was moved across the river on a barge to a sandy pine lot.

The cottage was built of durable cypress wood around 1924. It was unpainted when we moved in, had windows that were hung using ropes and weights, had old shutters, an aging roof and a sagging floor.

Not much to look at, but it was filled with charm and history, and we loved the old heart pine floors. It definitely had potential.

The property was filled with pines and sand spurs, which had tiny barbs that would cause pain if stuck into a finger or foot.

The barber's wife owned a little sewing business, making dresses and alterations on her foot-pedaled sewing machine, which was placed in one of the small front rooms. It was often frequented by customers arriving for all kinds of sewing needs. To this day there are pencil marks on the cypress walls to mark the sizes and heights of the various island ladies. (Just like the ones I had seen in Paris visiting the Dior designer workrooms.) The small room next to the one with the pencil marks became our guest room, putting a beautiful four-poster bed in it. After a few days we noticed that the floor in there acted like a trampoline and everything jiggled terribly when we giddily hopped up and down. We bribed a friend with homemade cookies to crawl into the narrow gap under the house, defying black snakes and who knows what else, only to find that, when the house was moved from the island to here, they had neglected to support that part! A few concrete blocks took care of that.

We fell in love with the little cottage and our magical life began.

We could hear the sea from our porch and the church bells in the evening on the island across the river. There were nesting owls in the ancient oak tree at the edge of the property and a nest of baby woodpeckers in the Jacaranda tree. We hung our hammock there for afternoons of reading and snoozing. Ed and I discovered a way of life that brought us joy and happiness in the solitude of the garden. We created a thicket of wild and native plants, giving refuge to wildlife, a natural place of beauty and seasonal colors. It has never been sprayed with poison, giving it a natural balance.

Living in Osprey Cottage is like a rich tapestry made of many colored threads. We created a vegetable and flower garden and a sleeping porch, so that we could dream in the magnificence of the moonlight. We surrounded ourselves with a nature sanctuary. Rabbits, armadillos and possums came to live in the refuge, along with squirrels and raccoons. Butterflies sailed in and out of the sunshine. Bees and birdsong brought a sense of peace.

You might think that all these scenes and happenings are taking place on a big parcel of land, when in reality it is barely one acre, lovingly tended.

Living in a house of history gives a sense of belonging and stability. It is a safe harbor and a place to put down roots, a place to create happy memories, a place to have a happy childhood.

How fortunate we are.

Monarch Butterfly

By Ilse

Zebra Longwing,
Florida's State Butterfly

By Suzanne

Remembering Ed

Ed was a true leprechaun and he was happiest when dressed in his green outfit on St. Patrick's Day. It consisted of an Irish green T-shirt, depicting a fiddling, red-haired gnome and a pot-o-gold under a rainbow. He donned a blinking bow tie and a tall top hat with a sprouting daisy. His knee socks were decorated with shamrocks, he wore shamrock shaped glasses, green curled-toe shoes and various other embellishments of shamrock pins, watches and rings.

Even his old 1979 VW camper was painted green and he named it "Shamrock".

Naturally he and his van were often recognized around town by smiling, pointing people. When Ed ran out of gas (the gas gauge was faulty), the police would bring him home and drive away with a friendly wave.

Ed loved to ride in the Christmas parade dressed as an elf, and people would laugh and clap when he drove by.

But his biggest pleasure was singing "When Irish Eyes are Smiling" on St. Patrick's Day. He had a powerful tenor voice, hitting the high notes with great enthusiasm, and old folks homes, doctors offices (scheduled in advance), as well as numerous restaurants waited for him to appear and sing his big heart out! His favorite places were the Winn Dixie food store and Dr. Shriar's dental office.

Ed brought a bit of sunshine with him wherever he went, and people loved him, including me!

Ah, we miss him!

Ed Relaxing under the tree .....

Rabbits

We found a nest of brown marsh rabbits in the garden, hidden under a bush and happily making a home. In the evening a large fat one sat in the open field, quietly, nose twitching. Ed enjoyed watching her and was inspired to write this poem:

HAPPY HARES HOPPED HUMOROUSLY and HARMLESSLY across HAY HOUSED HILLSIDES, until HORRIFIC HELLISH HOUNDS HAILED by HOLLERING HORSEMEN HURRIEDLY and HOARSELY HOWLED in HORRENDOUS HORROR and HOT HASTE.

HARES, HOUNDS, HORSES HURLED HASTILY across HILLS and HEDGES until HOLES and HAVENS HELPED HARES to HIDE and HEAVE HEAVENWARD HAPPILY:
"We're hidden, we're home!"

AHHHHHHH!

Ed Briley

Music and Concerts
By Suzanne

As a child I lived in an old house filled with music.

Aunties played gospel hymns on the piano, Daddy and his cronies practiced their Dixieland skills on the banjo, and everyone sang.

My cousin had her own TV show at age 13, singing and playing piano.

My grandfather played the violin and mandolin. I stuck to the classics: playing Bach and Chopin on the piano.

Making music gave us riches and brought us together, and to this day I can't imagine my life without it.

As part of Osprey Cottage living, Ed and I made music a source of joy for ourselves and others. We invited friends and neighbors to a musical concert series, held on Sunday afternoons. Beautiful music of piano, violin and guitar drifted through the house.

No tickets to purchase! Just the pleasure of listening to local talents in a charming old cottage with creaking floors. One concert even featured a book review. Cookies and tea were served at the reception and everyone mingled and had a good time.

Over the years, there have been students from the Bible College practicing, children's lessons on our grand piano, and who can forget Ed singing "When Irish Eyes are Smiling" with great enthusiasm at our St.Patrick's Day parties.

Suzanne & Arla Mandilas

Paul Hamaty & Brandon Glick

House Concert

Gershwin Favorites

Katherine Warren
Pianist

Largo
Friends come to practice
chopin
PP
#
neighbors listen...
bach
Bach
learn and play
Mozart
AND Ed Sings
Boogie Book
children come
Handel
Haydn
"chopsticks"
andante
often there is music in Osprey cottage..
Concerts
INSIGHTS & SOUNDS
Elora walks for her lesson through the orchard.
music BAG
"Music is the" language of the soul
Beethoven
mf
Osprey Cottage Concert Series

Frog Music
By Suzanne

There is plenty to keep frogs happy at Osprey Cottage:

A poison free garden, leafy foliage, places to hide, little water baths and a delicious smorgasbord of bugs to eat.

A family of four tree frogs took residence behind a canvas painting hanging on the wall of the front porch. They remained undisturbed while peacefully snoozing in their tight quarters. As a result I have experienced close encounters of the frog kind, including Mr. Frog leaping down the back of my shirt as I walked through the front door.

A bit "frisky", I mused.

Another perched at regular times in the outdoor shower, hanging in a crevice above, ogling me with sparkling eyes. I continued to ignore him while bathing. "A peeping amphibian", I thought.

Still another found its way into the inside crotch area of my swimsuit as it hung to dry in the sea grape tree. Imagine what an extremely frightful experience it was when I put it on, because I had no idea what was squirming down there! I bet my screams could be heard miles away.

Not only do our frog residents make themselves known when you least expect it, they are also persistent. Another memorable evening was when long frog legs (with suction cup feet) flew through the open bedroom door from outside, only to disappear somewhere in the room.

In the middle of the night I suddenly woke up from a deep sleep and remembered that a visitor might be lurking nearby. Turning on the light, I looked up to the ceiling and there it was! Happily resting on a blade of the ceiling fan, looking down on me, ready to leap. Should I turn it on and give the little intruder a wild ride? Maybe that wasn't such a good idea. So I turned off the light and went back to sleep.

So much for frogs. We share the same garden, but please not the same house.

P.S. Does anyone have a good recipe for frogs legs?

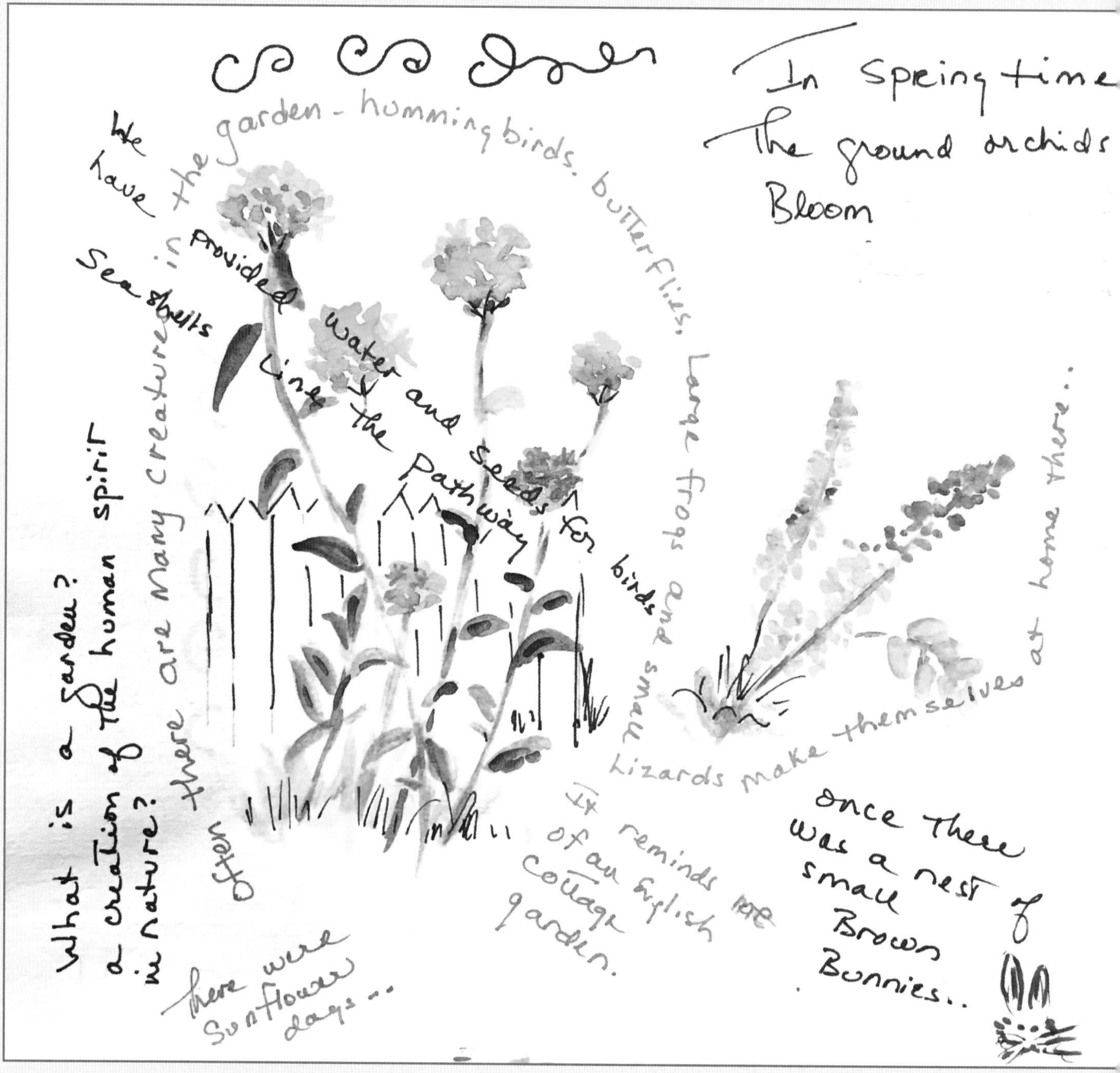

In Spring time
The ground orchids
Bloom

We have provided in the garden - hummingbirds, butterflies, Large frogs and small Lizards make themselves at home there...

Water and seeds for birds

Line the Pathway

Sea shells

What is a garden?
a creation of the human spirit
in nature?

there are Many creatures

Often

there were Sunflower days...

It reminds me of an English cottage garden.

once there was a nest of small Brown Bunnies..

Meet Hazel, a little clay chicken pot squatting on a table on the front porch, welcoming guests.

Happy Geraniums

The Garden
By Suzanne

Our love of nature guided Ed and me to create a garden full of great diversity. It sits in the middle of a fresh green thicket of wild coffee, necklace plants, palmettos, a variety of ferns, bananas, mangoes, sweet almond trees, strawberry guavas, Surinam cherries and pineapples. The ever reliable cocoplums fill the empty spaces.

During the winter our home-grown vegetables and herbs provide food for the table. Kale and lettuce are easy to raise in containers, using good soil and organic plant food. It's best to start with seedlings. We love the fresh greens but, unfortunately, so do aphids, an uninvited source of protein.

Tomatoes love the sun, and Malabar spinach will grow all year round, even in the summertime.

Our mulberry tree is filled with purple berries which birds love, and we enjoy watching them compete for the ripest ones.

Many colorful flowers in our garden attract all kinds of insects, 99% of which are beneficial. Butterflies sail by on their fluttering wings to bring a sense of magic.

A small plot is left alone, uncut, for wild grass gaillardias to reseed each year. They are a favorite of honey bees. Other flowers include geraniums, Panama roses, pentas, spiderwort, desert roses and poinsettias, a winter flower.

Our garden has a beautiful balance. We strive to have that balance in our lives.

The Vegetable Garden

Stupendous Sunflowers
By Suzanne

One summer Ed and I brought sunflower seeds home from England.

They came from our Victorian walled garden, where they had grown into jumbo sized flowers, and I decided that they would look wonderful in our Florida garden, if the climate agreed with them.

The seeds stayed in the refrigerator until ready to plant along our white picket fence in the front garden. It didn't take long and the seeds happily sprouted in the warm winter sun, growing to a height of 7 ft or more! They were majestic, with deep dark-brown centers, and the numerous petals of bright yellow-gold waved in the wind against a cobalt blue sky. What a beautiful sight!

Many people stopped their cars to take a closer look, asking to take photos. One of those even appeared in the local newspaper!

We didn't have the same grand results the following years. Maybe the seeds have to come from England? Another visit needs to be planned.

Yes! Anytime!

So many faces appeared along the fence —

Ed's favorite flower.. full of sunshine and happiness.

Our seeds were sold at the Treasure Coast Wildlife Hospital —

Jasmine of the night

Intoxicating fragrance

Riding the warm breeze

Ilse

Little mockingbird

Trilling treetop melodies

Tugging at my heart

Ilse

AMAZING BIRDS
By Ilse

How is it possible for the mockingbird to remember so many beautiful and diverse melodies?

Why does the nuthatch feed upside down?

I suspect a busy woodpecker is immune to headaches and back pain, and I smile.

How can a hummingbird, with its 70 wing beats per second, fly backwards or sideways?

Observations such as these have made me an avid birdwatcher. It enriches my life and the pleasure is totally free. Birds are fascinating!

Have you ever seen a male cardinal lovingly feed his mate during courtship?

Or watch birds and their antics in the birdbath?

The soaring birds of prey are amazing in their eyesight and speed needed for a successful hunt.

How can a tiny wren produce such a loud song?

What a thrill it is for me to identify a flitting warbler high up in the tree, which I have only seen in a bird book before.

You know you are too close to its nest when a mockingbird dive-bombs you with great courage and determination.

And when a bluejay screeches and jumps up and down, there probably is a cat nearby or a big fat crow.

I marvel at the mourning dove and its elegant shape. I enjoy the plaintive song and wonder why it is cocking its head back and forth all the time, and why the wings produce a high-pitched sound during flight.

I used to see so many more different bird species, but people don't like a wild, unkempt look in their yards, and so they prune every bush into a pleasing shape, spray against weeds and bugs, mow and blow, and in the process lose the diversity and survival of plants and animals, especially the birds.

MY FELLOW BIRDWATCHER
By Ilse

This well-weathered statue keeps me company when birdwatching,
which is one of my favorite pastimes.

I cut her rotund shape and her binoculars out of 3/4" oak, gave her some clothes using
outdoor paint and put a separate wooden cardinal on top of her cap,
fastened with a dowel so the bird can swivel.

So there she sits tenaciously watching, in heat or cold, in sun or rain, but unfortunately she
never tells me when she has an unusual or rare bird in her sights.

Could it be that the cardinal on her cap is really a scarecrow?

A little terra-cotta girl in the front garden is waiting patiently for a bird to come for a visit.

Meet Batz,
The guardian of the cottage.

Mulberry Muffins

Most cooks use blueberries for these muffins, but we add delicious mulberries, picked in a hurry from our tree next to the tiki hut, because the ever hungry birds, especially Mr. and Mrs. Cardinal, have discovered the sweet bounty as well.

Ingredients:

4 eggs

1 cup melted butter

2 cups sugar

2 cups sour cream

4 cups flour

2 tsp baking powder

1/2 tsp baking soda

1 tsp salt

2 cups mulberries

Mix eggs, butter, sugar and sour cream. Sift dry ingredients together, then add mulberries.

Fold berry/flour mix into the egg mixture until blended.

Spoon batter into well greased muffin tins and bake for 25 minutes in 375 degrees oven.

Makes 24 muffins.

Lavender

The scent of lavender in the garden on a crisp blue day with a gentle breeze and a slice of sunshine brings peace and calm to the mind.

Ed and I grow our lavender in containers in the springtime, before the summer heat arrives. As the tiny flowers bloom, I cut their long thin stems, tying them into bunches to store in the cupboard and between my bed sheets and pillow cases, where they last through the season, giving them a lovely fragrance. The flowers without the stems can be tied in handkerchiefs or colorful scraps of fabric, using satin ribbons or raffia string to give these little bundles a look of importance. I then hang them in my clothes closet.

Lavender may also be used in cooking. My favorite is lavender Creme Caramel, made by my granddaughter.

The word lavender comes from the Latin "lavare", meaning to wash. It was and still is used to perfume water for washing. Sprinkle your clothes with it before ironing.

Also: Cut it and place in water to root for propagation.

Rain Barrels

The heart of a vegetable garden is good soil and water.

The best pure water comes from rain.

Our rain barrels are attached to the gutters and have spigots.

We keep a variety of buckets and watering cans close by for easy use.

Rain water is also good for rinsing my hair and very practical for washing dogs.

The Jacaranda Tree

Lying in the hammock tied to our Jacaranda tree, it provides Ed and me with blue shade, and glimpses of soft, white clouds can be seen through its lacy leaves. A perfect place to read books.

Its blossoms are pale purple and seem to cover the whole tree when in bloom. It is sheer bliss when I fall asleep as the slight breeze kisses my toes. As sunset turns the sky peach and the evening air is diffused with the scent of lavender, it becomes a place of peace and magic.

Once, I opened my eyes to find six baby owls sitting on a limb above my head. They were practicing, learning how to fly.

A precious moment. Never to be forgotten.

One of God's many blessings.

On A Cold Morning....

Build a little fire outside, adding wood until a healthy flame licks the edges of the fire pit.

Invite some friends for breakfast and add comfy garden chairs around the fire to make a circle.

Give each guest a mug of coffee or tea as they arrive.

Be sure to keep the fire lively and warm, away from a strong wind and in a tucked-away corner of the garden.

Place your favorite pottery bowls on a small table nearby and serve hearty helpings of old-fashioned oat meal, steaming hot, with plump raisins, honey and a lashing of whiskey. Then watch everyone's cheeks flush pink with pleasure.

What fun!

A unique and creative way to share time and stories with neighbors and friends.

They won't want to leave...

SNOWBIRD
By Ilse

I lived in a country where winters were cold,
Where skies were dark grey and life seemed on hold.
I dreamed of a place of warmth and blue sky,
Of puffy white clouds looking down from up high,
Of palm trees and mangoes, of ocean waves mild...
Those visions were with me since being a child.

It took many years, made some turns that were wrong,
But now I am here and I feel I belong.
No boots and galoshes, thick gloves, coats of down,
I left them all back in a hurried, cold town.
Here I can breathe, and I dance in the sun,
My arms spread out wide, yes, life can be fun!

The storm came in fast

Will the palm trees keep bending?

And where are my birds?

Grey skies and light rain

Today I would welcome

A knock on the door.

Haikus - By Ilse

Marvelous Mangoes

When our mango tree starts producing ripening fruits in early summer, they come in with a vengeance!

We share that sweet, juicy, golden abundance with birds and squirrels, as well as with family, friends and neighbors.

Our kitchen is busy making:

Mango Nectar

Mango Chutney

Mango Cobbler

Mango Jam

Mango Daiquiris

There are Mango pieces in fruit salad

Mango in green salad

Mango in stir-fried chicken dishes

Mango in seafood recipes!

PLEASE, NO MORE MANGOES!

But in a short few weeks there are none left, and the prospect of buying them in the supermarket holds no excitement.

Mango Chutney

Ingredients:

4 mangoes, cubed

3 TBS grated fresh ginger

1 medium onion, finely chopped

1 large clove garlic, finely chopped

1/2 sweet red pepper, chopped

1/2 cup dark raisins

1/3 cup sugar

2 tsp salt

1/2 cup white vinegar

1/3 cup water

Combine all ingredients and slowly boil for 1 hour, stirring often.

Fill into sterilized jars.

Quick Mango Cobbler

Ingredients:

1/2 stick butter

1/2 cup flour

1/2 cup sugar

1 tsp baking powder

1/2 cup milk

Dash of salt

4 cups mangoes, cut up

Melt butter in overproof 9" casserole.

Mix flour, sugar, baking powder, milk and salt until smooth.

Pour over butter. Do not mix.

Heat fruit gently on stove and pour into casserole. Do not mix.

Bake at 350' until browned, approximately 20 minutes.

Surinam Cherries
(Sometimes called Star Cherry or Florida Cherry)
By Ilse.

Suzanne has a small tree of tart and tangy Surinam cherries in her backyard, but there is never enough fruit for jam making, because the cherries have one or more large seeds inside and you need a big basket full to make it worth your while.

Fortunately, I found an abundance of them on my Riverbend golf course, right next to the 18th tee, trimmed neatly to form a tall hedge. I asked one of my golfer friends to help me and she enthusiastically agreed, knowing that she would end up with a homemade jar of jam as a well-deserved reward.

We had to choose our sneaky "harvest time" carefully and with great stealth in order to avoid frustrated golfers, their errant tee shots and their interesting expletives.

The resulting jam tastes great on English muffins, and the "sneakiness" of it all makes it even more delicious!

Cocoplums
By Ilse

On a nature hike a few years ago, I came across some lush green bushes full of unfamiliar green, pink and deep purple fruit. I did some research and learned about the cocoplum, a resilient native of South Florida, which thrives in parks, coastal dunes, scrubland, golf courses and gardens. The purple fruit is edible and has almond-flavored seeds inside the pits, which can be roasted and munched on.

Recently I pulled into a parking lot and behold! There, of all places, was a thick row of cocoplum bushes loaded with fruit! Well, I am always tempted to make jam out of anything. I have used strawberries and blueberries picked on farms, Surinam Cherries pilfered from my golf course, mangoes from neighbors, crabapples and beach plums from Long Island, and now I had a new flavor. I grabbed my trusty basket and started picking. It's always the same story: pluck, mash, cook, enjoy and share a jar or two with grateful friends.

So if you should see a smiling lady with a blond pony tail in some parking lot, filling her basket with little purple globes from bushes, please don't worry: that's just me.

Ilse picking and plucking

VOILA!

Avocado Salad

Ingredients

    2 avocados, peeled and sliced

    1 lb shrimp, cooked and shelled

    4 cups watermelon, cubed

    1 small red onion, thinly sliced

    1/2 cup green grapes, cut in half (optional)

    1 Tbs cilantro, finely chopped

Place in large bowl and gently toss with Dressing.

Ingredients:

    3 Tbs olive oil

    1 Tbs honey

    Juice of 1 lime

Ilse

Sea Grape Jam

Sea grapes grow all along Florida's coast, and the tall bushes are distinguished by large heart-shaped leaves, woody stems and green and purplish berries, which can be made into delicious jam. Sea grapes cannot be purchased at markets, so this will require an authentic Florida outing to the beach. You'll want to choose the medium purple ones. Using a basket, comb your fingers over the grape clusters and the ripe ones should fall off easily.

Ingredients:

8 cups sea grapes
4 cups water
5 cups sugar
2 limes (1/4 cup juice)
1 box of Sure Jell pectin

In a large stainless steel pot, place the grapes and water and cook at medium heat for 1 1/2 hours, until the seeds begin to brake away from the fruit and the skins soften. Press with a potato masher to further loosen the fruit.

Place a mesh strainer in a large bowl, spoon the cooked grape mixture into the strainer and press, so that the juice and pulp drip into the bowl below. You will have around 4 cups. Add enough water to the mixture to make 5 cups total.

In a large pot bring the juice, pectin and lime juice to a rolling boil. Slowly add the sugar, stirring constantly. Bring the mixture to another boil for 1 minute.

Pour the hot jelly liquid into sterilized jars and seal tightly. Let it thicken overnight.

A yummy taste of Florida, delicious on a piece of fresh bread!

Suzanne Briley

Breakfast under the Carrotwood Tree .. each morning

The bicycle takes us to church, The Beach for saturday morning breakfast, to the market, friends to visit, and evening rides to the river.

Keep on rolling

Yes, Suzanne also wrote a monthly column in a local newspaper, covering current events and people. Here she told the readers about herself a few years back, describing not exactly a simple life.

One day in the story of my life

Hobe Sound Currents
June 2013

Suzanne Briley

Hopscotch

There is no way to describe my life but "zany." When I was growing up, I would open the fridge and the milk would automatically fall out, or open the medicine cabinet and the Mercurochrome would hit the white mosaic tile floor, spilling its bright orange contents into the cracks leaving a permanent stain. My life was always far from ordinary. It continues in Hobe Sound.

For instance, yesterday was a typical day: To start it off, there were loads of artists coming to paint in my barn (a weekly happening) with side shows. After mowing the grass in the garden, dragging out tables, putting up easels, sweeping the floor, moving the car and taking care of mother (age 99) tending to her needs, the barn filled with people starting to work. There was standing room only.

One artist brought her son, a retired banker. As therapy for his depression, he is painting on large palm fronds that fall out of trees. He is on heavy meds. Everyone encourages him. His friend silk screens shirts, paints on underwear and burial clothes.

I noticed that the person next to her proceeded to use charcoal to draw scenes of church interiors on large papers partly from memory. She has tremors. Next to her a person was gluing palm fronds on canvas and painting over them; another young woman who had a stroke was painting on canvas using only her fingers.

Someone was dying fabric, which was drying on my washing line, and my mother sat in the corner painting a portrait of her great grandson hanging out of a tree. Not far from her, there was an artist actually sitting up in my tree house, painting. There are more people coming in and out, some to watch and others to set up.

I leave them to fend for themselves and head out to the Hobe Sound Library to end my own solo painting exhibition there. I am to go and collect them by 11 a.m. I clean out my car to make space, but mother decides to abandon her portrait and ride with me. Now there is no room for my husband, Ed, to go along to help bring my pictures home. On the way out of the house, someone calls on the phone to buy a painting, and I tell her I will leave it in the library for her.

When I arrive at the library to leave the painting there that had just been purchased, carrying it along with me, I am told I can't leave it in the library. Mother is sitting in the hot car waiting for me, so I hurriedly accept the offer that a kind person makes to deliver a painting for me. Unfortunately, I have lost the person's telephone number who purchased the painting. I can't call her, so that doesn't work.

I rush home to find my bank on the phone (they have tried to reach me for two days, they said) and as I try to listen, I see my dog, Sophy, throwing up on the back porch. It is going down into the wood floor cracks. I call Ed for help, but he can't hear because he is deaf.

In the meantime I discover that Ed has taken two cycle racks from the barn and donated them to Goodwill (without asking me) and neither one of them are ours. I rush to collect them before it is too late but they are gone.

Mother needs some cards mailed, but we are out of stamps. I hurry to the post office while everyone in the barn is waiting for me to return so we can all eat lunch together under the tree. There are not enough chairs so I try and find some, just as my ex-husband calls to say he is bringing some books by to leave. I tell him to leave them on the front porch, because there is no place for him to park.

The county comes to trim the trees along the road, and my car is in the way and has to be moved. Back in the barn, the bi-polar man has used the toilet, and I know he didn't shut the lid and vermin might appear. (There are worries in my mind!)

Mother announces to everyone that she and I will play a piano duet and invites everyone to come inside. (Ed is trying to take a nap in the other room.) Just then a real estate broker knocks on the front door to ask if the house is for sale. (He heard it might be?) We invite him in to listen to the duet.

Mother and I give a stellar performance, and as people start to leave, the recycle truck arrives requiring me to rush outside and move my car. Again. When I come back inside the phone is ringing. It is the woman calling about not finding her painting she was supposed to collect in the library. I arrange to take it to Steinmart and meet her there in the car park on Saturday. As we speak I see Sophy throwing up on the carpet. (She goes to the vet tomorrow.) I clean up the barn and find that someone has left their clothes in my studio, the books are on the front porch and a notice has appeared about a dock we built in Tequesta 12 years ago.

I invite Mother, Ed and friend, Dot, to go to Taste restaurant for dinner (where I used up the last of my credit), but Mother said that Dot talked too much because she drank three glasses of wine. I only drank one, but felt like I could have finished off a whole bottle! We came home and Mother and I watched an old video from the library. A Russian film about 12 chairs. I fell sound asleep on the sofa. Mother was still going strong at 11 p.m.

Tomorrow she packs to go home to Atlanta without knowing that Sophy has chewed a hole in her travel case. It will be another day for me... ■

Suzanne Briley, who lives in Hobe Sound, is an artist, author, entrepreneur, environmentalist and world traveler. She may be contacted at hopscotch@hscurrents.com.

BOOKS EVERYWHERE

What would Osprey Cottage be without books!

They stand straight on a shelf like soldiers, or lean sideways like old sots. The large, treasured art books are stacked up horizontally and never have a chance to collect dust.

Books finds themselves in a bathroom, in a study, on a coffee table, and some are sitting by the front door waiting to be returned to the library.

A cookbook lies open on the kitchen counter. A book of prayer has a place on a bedside table. A favorite novel, sent by a friend, is ready for the hammock or the beach bag. Familiar old text books with well-worn pages, classics, music books, photo albums and written memories, some from childhood, are all well loved and bring times of quiet and reflection as we turn their pages.

During this time of electronic communication, information and eBooks we have unending possibilities and availability. But lost is the comfort of looking at a wall of books, which makes any room feel cozy. The knowledge of an old, hand-written recipe in that cookbook on the counter. Being able to hold an actual photo from an album in your hand or leafing through your favorite art book.

That is irreplaceable.

Ilse

Baskets
By Suzanne

Our barn is filled with baskets of all shapes, colors and sizes. Hanging from the wall on long nails, ready for use. For laundry, garden clippings and flowers, firewood, fruit and vegetables, bread, eggs and pies for picnics. Dogs and cats love to sleep in baskets. My friend in Holland used one for her baby to sleep in. It had a tiny mattress filled with soft ferns from the forest. Baskets are handy for magazine and newspaper storage, for picking berries, oranges, mushrooms or nuts. At times they are even used for storing bottles of wine, as in the following story:

My friends were on a holiday in a remote part of Spain. They were driving a car, with two children and their grandma in the back seat.

Suddenly, in the middle of nowhere, granny had a heart attack and died. Unable to leave her in the car with the children, they placed her in a large wine basket they were carrying with them, removing the bottles and covering her with a blanket.

They then tied her carefully and securely to the top of the car and made their way slowly north to find help. They were in anguish, crying and upset.

At last finding a place for assistance they parked the car, leaving the wine basket on top, and went inside. Since they spoke no Spanish, it took some time to explain their situation. When the family finally returned to the car, much to their surprise and shock, they found the basket was gone!

Thieves had no wine, but they had grandma. She was never found.

FIRE WOOD

BERRIES

FRUIT

LAUNDRY

FLOWERS

TEA POTS

Tea With Lemonade

Cold tea in a Thermos

Tea in a Tent

Tea With The Queen

One Lump or Two?

Hot Tea in Bed

Tea Under a Tree

Sugar

Tea With Gin

Teapots
By Suzanne

As the sun rises in the early morning, the steam from our tea pot also rises, as if to say 'hello' to the new day. As always in the old cottage with the creaky wood floors and four poster bed, tea is served. Smoky Lapsang Souchong, steeped in a choice of tea pots on a little tray with a slice of toast and home-made mango jam is a delight. Never mind the crumbs.

In the stillness of the day's beginning one can think quietly and plan the day ahead. An old, faded quilt tucked around the knees helps to provide a sense of security and comfort.

My favorite tea varieties include Constant Comment spiced tea, peppermint, chamomile, red rooibos (African bush tea), or just plain old green or black tea. Hibiscus tea is delicious and simple to make, as you can see from the following recipe on page 62. Drink it hot or keep it in the refrigerator, ready for a sweltering summer day. Fill a thermos with it to take along on a hike or picnic.

There are teas for stomach aches, colds, nausea, sore throats, sleeplessness and more. You have a choice of hundreds of teas from all over the globe, and steeping these in a pretty pot makes it special.

Tea pots can be story tellers. They originated in China centuries ago. They were used to hold the crushed leaves of the tea plant and became not only necessary but fashionable in their elegant beauty of Chinese porcelain making.

I have been collecting tea pots for a long time and I am fond of every one of them. They fill shelves, stand in cupboards, decorate a mantel piece or take a place of pride in a china cabinet.

A favorite is a sitting camel made out of porcelain. Its long neck and head are the pouring spout and an Arab sheik rides on the back. Just imagine sitting in a large tent in the deserts of Jordan, a massive fire warming the cold night and camels and their riders circled around for warmth, music and conversation. Brilliant diamond stars light a black sky path, and tea made from sage wafts its scent in gentle waves, locking a lasting memory in one's heart. My camel tea pot is from that time.

Then there is my Brown Betty from England, a classic. Made of shiny brown pottery, well loved and remembered, it has a long history of warming our hands and insides during the cold, misty British days of winter. During the time we spent on our long-distance walks in England, a Brown Betty pot filled with steaming tea was usually my reward at rest stops. The one in my collection is a large fat one, bringing back all those memories, with tales to tell.

There also are fine bone China pots of Wedgewood, Royal Doulton and Havilland with thin, translucent sides and gold designs. We only use these pieces for a special afternoon tea in the cottage dining room.

Parts of the family once lived in the Dutch East Indies for a while, and when they returned to their home in Argentina, they brought with them beautiful antique blue and white Chinese oriental porcelain sets from a tea plantation. I went to visit them and was honored to be served tea from their ancient set. When they realized how much I admired it, they kindly gave the tea pot to me to take home, where it stands safely on a shelf in the china cabinet, much treasured.

Also in the collection is a 'Hotel Silver' pot, which looks like silver but really isn't, and an 'English' one which is. An indestructible stainless-steel one is for picnics.

But above all my pieces, my lettuce tea pot stands out the most. A lovely translucent shade of green, it is handmade by well known Florida ceramist Dodie Thayer. A mother of five, Dodie arranged her time, talents and life to produce her unique and beautiful pieces in her kiln at home. They sold quickly on Worth Avenue in Palm Beach, and eventually were found in exclusive collections throughout the world, including the Queen of England, Barbara Sinatra, Brooke Astor, Duchess of Windsor, Jackie Onassis and many others. Her famous and expensive lettuce ware is featured in countless magazines and papers. It was recently shown in a retro exhibition at the Lighthouse Art Gallery in Tequesta, Florida. I am proud to have her exquisite tea pot in a special place, a large window surrounded by soft green Florida foliage. A perfect background for this work of art.

And then there are some others in unique shapes and sizes, fun to look at and delightful in my collection, including a gas can, cow, fire truck, red bird and a woman's fancy hat box!

Actually, anything can be a tea pot as long as you find a suitable spot to place a pouring spout!

And a lid.....

often during the winter
months, Ed and I enjoy tea
amongst the flowers in the
cottage garden.. near the
young Gumbo limbo tree.

Suzanne

Hibiscus Tea

Make the tea with either fresh or dried flowers and choose to have it as a hot cup of tea or as hibiscus iced tea. Either way, it's delicious, has a beautiful deep pink hue and is really good for you.

Ingredients:

2 cups fresh hibiscus flowers (or 1/2 cup dried ones)

8 cups water

1/4 cup honey (add more for extra sweetness)

3 Tbs lime juice

If using fresh flowers, remove the green parts at the base of the flower.

Bring the hibiscus and water to a boil in a large pot. Once the water starts boiling, remove from heat and cover the pot. (At this point you can add other herbs such as basil, lemon grass, lemon zest or mint) Let it steep for 15 - 20 minutes. Strain the tea and mix in the honey and lime juice.

Suzanne

Tree Loft

Tree Loft
By Suzanne

A magical place!

The old shrub oak tree stands majestically in the back corner of the garden, spreading its arms out wide to provide a great canopy of shade.

It is 55 feet wide and touches two other property lines. My botanist friend said it is the largest one in the area. Sturdy stairs, built by my friend Martin (who later appeared on TV's Shark Tank as a designer of tree houses), lead me to a world of high views and cool green leaves.

An aerie!

Early in the morning the light chases gray battleship clouds across the sky.

The old tree represents life itself:

Many broken branches, scars, unwanted lichen, dead beginnings and vulnerable to storms, offering the present, remembering the past.

Scattered shade, birds, geckos, squirrels.

Holy silence.

Survival.

God's creatures are at hand.

What a special spot to read, pray, connect with nature.

This is how we live a simple, yet rich life, happily in the tree!

But it is not always so bucolic in that wondrous tree loft, where birds and Beaujolais mingle, as you can see on the following page.

One fine evening some friends of a rather corpulent nature had a jolly good time up there, sipping wine and laughing at my jokes. The sun started to set and it was mosquito time. My bare legs under the little table became the target of a skeeter feeding frenzy. I kept quiet, mistakingly hoping that soon everyone would leave.

Perhaps my large lady friend was afraid to squeeze down the somewhat narrow stairs. After all, it is a lot easier climbing up than teetering down, especially after imbibing a healthy amount of vino.

At last, someone felt the call of nature and the little party filed down the stairs. Unfortunately, my rotund friend missed some of the last steps, went flying with a wail and landed on her ample, well-cushioned bum.

With a little help she got back on her feet, laughing tears.

I was laughing with her, greatly relieved, because she was a lawyer.

We only occasionally run into each other these days. She sometimes mentions her nagging back ache, and I have noticed a slight limp.

I cringe.

There are now new tree loft rules in place:

NO MORE THAN 1 1/2 GLASSES OF WINE/CHAMPAGNE PER PERSON!

Our beloved tree loft has many other uses besides
observing and connecting with nature:

In the Tree

Wine Parties
Birthdays
Tea in the afternoon
a Wedding -
Marriage proposal
Strawberry Sundaes +
home made cookies
Breakfasts
Dinners
Signing of important
papers!
Fortune Telling ???
Music

Henrietta's Birthday Cake

This is grandma Henrietta's special cake, served on her 100th BIRTHDAY!

Over the years many birthdays have been celebrated at Osprey Cottage. Grandma's coconut cake is the very favorite. Everyone waits for a second helping and for the recipe.

On the day we celebrated her very own 100th birthday in the cottage garden, we decorated the top of the white cake with fresh, deep-red bougainvillea flowers. It was beautiful to look at and heavenly to eat.

And now we are sharing the recipe once again!

Ingredients:

1 package white cake mix

2 cups sour cream

2 cups confectioners sugar

12 ozs. shredded coconut

14 ozs. Whipped cream

Dash of vanilla

Prepare the batter according to package directions. Bake at 350 degrees in 2 9inch pans, let cool and split each cake in half, making 4 layers.

While cake is baking, combine sour cream, sugar and coconut (saving some to sprinkle over top later) and refrigerate.

Spread this mix between the layers. Cover cake with whipped cream/vanilla and sprinkle with remaining coconut.

Decorate with fresh flowers or ferns from the garden.

Gardenias
By Ilse

How lovely they smell when they finally bloom!

I pick some from the bush and float the short-stemmed blossoms in an heirloom crystal bowl, so that we can enjoy their sweet fragrance during dinner.

The next morning, all we find is a drooping brown bouquet, not fit to share our breakfast table.

It was wonderful while it lasted.

Quilts, Mugs, Jugs and a Quaint Old Bath Tub

A quilt on a four-poster bed makes a statement in an old cottage.

It adds a sense of coziness, color and comfort. A 'One Quilt Night' or 'Two Quilt Night' or 'Three Quilt Night' for warmth. Ours are lovingly hand-sewn, with beautiful designs, and are passed down through the family. A really special one was stitched on a white quilted background and embroidered by children in 1920!

Bowls, plates, mugs and cups fill the shelves and cupboard, adding color and cheer to the kitchen and dining area. Some are souvenirs from days of travel, others are flea market finds or inherited family pieces and gifts. Blue and white, rosy red, harvest gold, and green lettuce ware bring interest and history to the room. A table set with unmatched pottery and colorful mugs and jugs bring joy, fun and even conversation to any outside table in the garden. Large sea grape leaves can be used for place mats.

In addition to outdoor showers under the trees, with the blue sky overhead, our cottage also has a claw foot bathtub. Filled with steamy hot water up to the chin, it is a place to dream and relax before bed.

On some special nights, a large silver moon peeks through the window.

It is magic.

Suzanne

Local Characters
By Suzanne

Living in a cottage has the advantage of a front porch for comfy sitting, perhaps in a rocking chair, and, unless the trees and shrubs have grown too tall, one can look at people passing by without them even noticing you.

Our neighborhood certainly has its share of funny and interesting characters who think nothing of flaunting their peculiarities and eccentricities in public, and I enjoy every one of them.

Here are a few favorites of mine:

A man dressed in a Tyrolean outfit, white shirt, colorful suspenders, leather shorts, white knee socks in sandals, and a jaunty feather flying from his hat, as he and his lady friend strolled by. She was a vision in her own right. She wore a see-through dress in a leopard print.

A fine pair!

Another time a woman cycled by. It was early morning and she wore her pink nightie with dark pink flamingos on it, hair in curlers and fuzzy, pink slippers. She was belting out "God Bless America ", Ethel Merman style!

Thinking back and remembering other characters, there are two that definitely stand out.

One of them was a very tall, thin, Gandhi-like man with a shiny bald head, no shirt covering his scrawny chest, wearing only a black thong, riding a unicycle. The sun reflected as bright as a mirror on his head as he flew around the block.

His girl friend, "Muscle Margaret", followed behind on her own unicycle. Her attire consisted of skimpy red shorts and a sleeveless white undershirt, exposing and showing off her massive, rippling muscles among her other, voluptuous, pendulous attributes. A happy, grinning face caused her to be noticed by everyone as she gave the sign of peace, whizzing by.

On another occasion, I remember a large black car driving past, and something unusual about it caught my attention. The rear had been cut out to make room for a black wood burning stove! The smoke pipe was sticking up out of the side window. In the front, next to the driver, sat a tall brown llama going along for a ride! They both looked happy.

And then here was this massive, noisy garbage truck driving around and around the Zeus Park circle. When the driver was finally asked if he needed help or was lost, he replied 'Oh, no'. He was just practicing his driving skills.

A familiar and favorite sight was Harry, owner of "Harry and the Natives" (a local restaurant and pub), zooming around neighborhood streets in his comfortable, motorized arm chair! Cherry red, plush and large, it would swivel and glide at a safe speed so that everyone was able to get a good look at this contraption. His face was happy, and more often than not he would have two children with him, one curled under each arm, enjoying the ride.

Perhaps the most unusual of this colorful collage of local characters was a woman strolling along Bridge Road in the middle of the day. She was walking a small white pony which had a lot of brown spots on its body. They were ' Look A Likes', because the woman was attired in a white dress which ALSO had lots of brown spots on it! What a pair!

Wonders never cease!

I never said all characters in the neighborhood were lovable:

I was suspicious from the moment the new neighbor moved in. Who in the world would paint a house deep purple like a giant eggplant, with lime-green squares and polka dots around the front door and a swinging monkey above the window! She also owned a mean little dog who enjoyed barking, chasing and nipping.

I love to ride my bike and it takes me to the dentist, doctor, drugstore, and at day's end on a leisurely glide downhill to the river.

As I cycled past the purple house one day, there she was, the new neighbor on her porch, looking like the Wicked Witch of the West with a personality to match, as I soon found out. And her dog was a chip of the Old Crock. That small ball of flying fur came running after me, yapping and catching up fast. I placed my feet up on the handle bar and tried to coast along, hoping the little beast would give up the chase, but no such luck. The bike slowed, my feet came down and my ankle got attacked by sharp little teeth.

"Lady, please call off your dog!" I shouted.

"It's his front yard. Go ride another street!" the woman snarled back, unfazed and uninterested.

Similar encounters between me and the mutt followed.

I am a firm believer in 'Love Thy Neighbor', which probably includes the neighbor's dog. So next time, when that mean dust mop charged off the porch again, I suddenly stopped my bike and the dog skidded to a halt. I quickly reached down and offered a yummy dog biscuit. 'Peace be upon you', I smiled. The dog snatched up its treat, chomped it down and promptly proceeded to sink its teeth into my ankle!

Yikes! This time it drew blood! I hurled a curse and pedaled home to apply some disinfectant.

A few days later I was hobbling through the pet supplies section of our local supermarket when they beckoned to me... a lovely display of Vet's Best GAS BUSTERS, delicious chewable tablets for constipation, gas and bloating.

Hmmmm.

Next day I biked past the purple house at a faster clip. Sure enough, the mutt spotted me and launched off his porch. I quickly dropped two little Gas Busters on the ground and sped away, seeing the dog wolfing them down.

I waited for results. The following day I rode by the house of the Wicked Witch and noticed a van parked in front:

SPENCER'S RUG AND UPHOLSTERY CLEANING.

No dog in sight as I pedaled on peacefully.
Sometimes revenge can be so sweet. Literally.

(A few months later, the mean duo moved away and the house was repainted a boring beige.)

The Banyan Tree
By Ilse

There it is, just around the corner from Osprey Cottage, spreading its huge limbs and sending down many feelers to the ground in order to start new tree trunks. An endless growing cycle, unless held in check by pruning.

Sitting on a bench in its deep shade makes me and my problems seem insignificant, and I luxuriate in the tree's grandeur.

Bravado
By Ilse

The gecko is looking at me

As if I don't live here, you see.

"It's my place and therefore how dare you!

I'll show you my neck patch to scare you!"

He flashes his bright orange throat

In hopes that I frighten and bolt.

Such courage for someone so small.

He continues to climb up the wall...

Chicken Scratchings
By Suzanne

Often chickens are part of cottage life, supplying fresh eggs or ending up as the main ingredient in delicious soup. They can become pets or pests.

One day my neighbor installed a wall of wooden laying boxes along the fence between us. There were 27 chickens under my bedroom window!

Very, very close. Before long a rooster showed up and began the busy task of roostering. After a few pre-dawn announcements awakening the neighborhood he was sent away to a farm out of town.

The remaining 27 hens began their happiness at laying eggs. They became "egg-sperts " at producing white, brown and light blue colored eggs. There were cackles, screeches, scratchings (often on my side of the fence), and chicken odors. My days were less than peaceful. There were just too many of them!

After a while, desperate and not wanting to upset my neighbor by complaining, I silently thought: Perhaps they would enjoy a ride in my bicycle basket, one at a time. They loved it! Cuddled under a tea towel, a short ride took them to a posh neighborhood where I released each one quietly, hoping that they would be lovingly treated as pets. I don't think my neighbor missed the few I took, but for me there were less cackles in my life.

Actually, I began being introduced to chickens at an early age.

My grandmother's cottage in the heart of the countryside, with a large garden of English peas, carrots, tomatoes, corn, lettuce and pear trees, had a chicken yard as well.

My sister Nancy and I often spent summers with her. My then eight-year-old sister loved chickens, but I was frightened of them as they puffed themselves up, screeched, and with yellow, flashing eyes chased after me, trying to peck my bare legs. I remember running away, terrified of the attack.

One day Nancy tried on Mother's engagement ring, just for fun. It had a beautiful diamond but was much too large for a child's finger. We all forgot she was wearing it when she went outside to feed the chickens, tossing corn around the yard, far and wide. A hungry platoon of fowl sped out to peck, grab and gobble up the tasty morsels.

Later, in the house, Mother asked for her ring, but it was too late: it had disappeared from Nancy's finger. Of course it was nowhere to be seen in the chicken yard. A chicken had become engaged?

A long, long while later we heard that, as chicken dumplings were being prepared in the kitchen, a diamond ring appeared inside a chicken's tummy!

Mother was delighted, and today it shines forth on Nancy's finger.

Exiled but still Strutting!
By Ilse

Please, not at five in the morning!

Cranky, lean and spent, those tough old roosters are perfect for the following recipe:

ROOSTER (Chicken) SOUP
By Ilse

Ingredients

1 scrawny rooster, skin on

3 large carrots, peeled and cut into big chunks

5 stalks of celery, cut in half

2 large yellow onions, peeled and halved

1 bay leaf

Optional: whole peppercorns, garlic cloves, parsnips, fennel bulb, leeks

In a large pot cover the chicken with water and gently simmer for 2 hours, skimming off any foam.

During the last hour of cooking add the bay leaf and vegetables.

Carefully remove chicken and vegetables and let cool. Pour the broth through a strainer and return to pot.

Pull the meat off the bones, discarding them and the skin. Chop the meat and vegetables and return to the broth. Season with salt and pepper and reheat.

Ladle into bowls and garnish with chopped parsley.

Optional: pre-cook noodles or rice separately and add to soup.

The Washing Line
By Suzanne

Blue sky
A day for the washing line
Bra and knickers
Hang upside down

Towels and sheets
Snap to attention to join the dance
A scent of clean
A line to enchant

Dazzling white
A shirt on its side
A skirt stands upright

Socks, cases, squares and round
Flying as you please
High above the ground

Wind whirls and flows
Magic comes and goes
Threads, buttons and hems
Tangle, flap and clap

Yellow, red and blue
In sunlight fresh
A suit, a blouse, a dress

A basket stands waiting
For soon they will dry
And come indoors again
Away from the sky

A life of their own
Freedom to express!
Oh, to be on the washing line
A life of MY own
Freedom to fly!

Jokesters vs. Pranksters
By Suzanne

I never could understand why they are called "practical jokes", when most pranks are highly ridiculous, often quite crude and all of them decidedly impractical.

But I love them, and I firmly believe that a bit of humor is like a pinch of salt added to food: it brings out the flavor. Which is one big reason I was drawn to Ed, he of the same affliction.

In my case it must be hereditary, because my father was also an incorrigible jokester. It was he, partner in a stuffy law firm, who gave me and my friends a ride to school wearing a Marilyn Monroe wig, just to name one of his many pranks.

As fate would have it, Ed and I ran into some serious competition when we moved into the cottage. Our next-door neighbor was a puckish, playful sort of fellow, so he became our prime suspect when we came home one day after a week-long absence to find a FOR SALE sign on our front lawn. Luckily, it had a small SOLD notice on the bottom, but that only triggered a wave of phone calls from neighbors asking where we were moving.

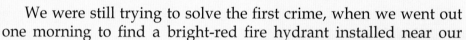

We were still trying to solve the first crime, when we went out one morning to find a bright-red fire hydrant installed near our mailbox. Before we could retaliate, we found a dark-brown wooden horse head poking out of the hedge behind our picket fence. By this time we suspected that other neighbors had enlisted in the Prankster-in-Chief's army, because the horse head suddenly sported dreadlocks and a joint stuck in his mouth. During Halloween he acquired a vampire hat and for Christmas a white Santa

Claus beard. We loved hearing the laughter from people passing by.

Ed and I held a war council and decided on an aggressive strategy that the Air Force would have called carpet bombing.

It began by placing an old toilet in our dear neighbor's front yard, lid up, right between two lawn chairs and some shrubs.

Next, I stretched a long clothes line between some palm trees, also in his front yard. I pinned up colorful underwear, pants and nighties, all in size 'extra large'. They were nicely swinging in the breeze on a bright sunny day when he drove in from work. Neighbors called him to ask if he needed a clothes dryer.

After that, I wrapped the front of his house with crime tape.

Creative jokes consumed our thinking for a while. Among my ideas were a sign: "Free Puppies", another one read: "Horseback Riding Lessons" (phone number included).

Still another appeared on the back of his truck: "Just Married".

Any interesting object that I needed to throw away would turn up somewhere on his property. In a tree a plastic owl, pots and pans to make a border around his mailbox. Old screens, boxes, an unwanted piano - they all found a new home in his side yard.

Finally, I remembered a prank which was one of my father's favorite!

I put a smoke bomb under the hood of the neighbor's truck, giggling and feeling gleeful. Since the driveway was right next to his house, I had to wait for an opportune time to remain undetected while doing the deed. When the poor unsuspecting man turned the ignition switch, the action began! A loud explosion sent massive clouds of smoke into the air, billowing out from under the hood. Of course it looked much worse than it really was, but what fun to watch it all from a safe distance.

Later, we realized that the practical joker had some ideas of his own again, and they were quite clever.

A unadorned clothes mannequin appeared on our front steps, staring "nakedly" at passers by.

A "Poop Factory" for dogs was discovered. It was home-made from card board and black pipes.

Walking the dog one day I found my name emblazoned on a park table: "Suzanne Slept Here".

And he got us with a really good one: An old car lived in our driveway. It was meant to be a crime deterrent and it never moved, because it didn't run.

What a surprise one day when, sticking out from under its side, a male dummy appeared to be working on the old clunker. He was wearing jeans, boots and work gloves, tools and a beer can stood ready for use, making the scene truly authentic looking. He remained there for a long time, becoming a convenient and efficient part of a home security system. Many people stopped by for a chat, thinking he was real, and even I got in the habit of talking to him while passing by.

My next and last prank, a magnificent idea, would be to call a mover and have his house moved somewhere else. Perhaps out of the neighborhood? If only I could find a company to do it for a reasonable price.

HMMMMMMM

The Barn

The cottage has a very large barn, which was once a place for building boats.

Now it is used for many activities, but mostly for art projects. Its lofty ceiling and wide open doors and windows make it the perfect home to inspire a diversity of paintings in various media, and an eclectic array of other projects, such as painting furniture, making quilts, and painting coconuts, stones, baskets, even old doors to create colorful "masterpieces ".

We have lunch together under the thatched roof of the adjacent tiki hut, discuss our work and inspire each other. Then it is back to creating, often painting for charity and art sales, which are at times held right there in the driveway.

Over a period of years we became known as "The Barn Artists" in various newspaper and magazine articles, and the list of our charity work became lengthy, as our paintings were donated to our community and beyond. There was Hibiscus House Children's Shelter, Treasure Coast Wildlife Hospital, Audubon of Martin County, Humane Society, Art for Peace, War and Peace Museum and the Hobe Sound Mural Art project, founded by Nadia Utto, a non-profit organization which serves 21 towns in Florida promoting the rich history of an outside art gallery.

Several Barn Artists joined up to teach art to residents and shut-ins at a local assisted living center, sharing their talents and skills and bringing joy to the elderly.

The barn is surrounded by mature trees and a flowering garden. The large bougainvillea bushes leaning over the white fence are a constant joy and an object of many paintings, making it a center of great energy.

The barn was once blessed by a priest from India. It was used for yoga instructions, children's art classes, practice area for an Irish band, healing services, and a 100th birthday party. It was even used for a small motorcycle convention!

Mural Art

**New Life
for
Old Pieces**

Inspiration
By Ilse

As soon as I joined the Barn Artists, my creative juices began flowing like an untamed mountain stream. My main medium as an artist is watercolor, and since I am an avid bird watcher, they are often my chosen subjects. But I also love to paint children at the beach in all their innocence and exuberance. It has always been a source of great pleasure and satisfaction to make vibrant colors flow on paper.

But now I started to get inspired to work in other media as well. I created colorful fish by cutting them out of left-over pieces of 2X4 or 2X6 construction lumber retrieved from a neighborhood dumpster, and the Barn Artists and I gave old furniture a new lease on life by painting them with flowers and landscapes.

Since I love walking the ocean beaches picking up interesting rocks and shells, I began creating little undersea worlds by glueing these onto framed, painted pieces of plywood, calling them "Stoned Fish". I find these beach "treasures" on my many travels: the Red Sea and North Sea, the Pacific and Atlantic, the Baltic and Caribbean, and each piece comes with memories and images attached, which makes it so much fun to place them just right on my collage.

Then somehow I got the idea of painting dried-out coconuts to resemble fish, and other artists joined in. We used palm fronds for fins and tails, and the creases in the coconuts gave the fish the funniest and quirkiest of expressions. Soon I was running low in my supply, when luck would have it I found a pile of brown, dried coconuts by the side of the road, ready for garbage pickup. I happily loaded them into my car, but driving away I noticed an awful, pungent smell emanating from my newly-found treasure. I think neighborhood dogs had found the pile attractive as well, had lifted their legs and marked their territory!

I haven't painted a coconut since.

Maybe I should stick to my beloved watercolors?

"Stoned Fish"

Coconuts
By Ilse

The Barn Artists had a lot of fun painting coconuts to resemble colorful fish. We hung some of them in the gazebo under the thatched roof, where they dangled over our heads watching, as we artists poured ourselves a well-deserved glass of wine.

In other words:

One day we painted some coconuts

And hung them up high in the tiki hut.

As we swizzled good wine, glasses swirled,

Above us those funny globes whirled,

Ere long we felt like some loco nuts!

Yarn from the Barn
By Ilse

Once a week we come together
To plan and paint, birds of a feather.
So there we are, a motley lot,
The doors wide open, 'cause it's hot.
And light comes in, so does a breeze,
Creative juices flow with ease.
The bugs and skeeters sometimes come,
A little spritz - and they are done.
We see the flowers, hear the birds,
The geckos peek at us with mirth,
But "Batz", our dog, is on the prowl
And chases them with quite a howl.

We start in earnest: Draw the sketch,
There is no time now for a kvetch.
We mix the paints, we prime the brush,
Apply the careful strokes, no rush.
We scratch our heads an awful lot:
Should I use red, or maybe not?

We barely like what we create.
So we encourage: "WOW, that's great"!
"It's beautiful ", "I like the scene",
"The mood's just right", (know what I mean?).
Well, yes, I know, we lie a tad
And thus avoiding feeling bad.

We work quite hard, this diverse bunch,
Until it's time to go have lunch.
The tiki hut is where we eat,
A shady, wonderful retreat.
We laugh, inspire and have fun,
Until the sandwiches are done.

Then back we go to paint some more,
Good painting light shines through the door.
Soon we get kissed by our Muses,
And they ignite artistic fuses.
Oh masterpieces! Here they come!
So just you wait until they're done.
And then we pray: Will Lady Luck
Please help us to bring in big bucks?
But no, alas, we all stay poor.
Great Rembrandts we are not, for sure.

Gorgeous Bougainvilleas thrive next to the barn, delighting everyone.

MEET A FEW OF THE BARN ARTISTS!

Margaret Gray

After careers as a laboratory and X-ray technician, floral designer and flower shop owner, Margaret turned to painting to express her artistic vision. Having studied with many nationally renowned artists, and mastering the mediums of watercolor, acrylic and oil, Margaret now paints primarily in oil.

She is a signature member of the National Oil and Acrylic Society and the recipient of the Arts Council Marties award for Visual Artist in 2005.

She has participated in juried solo and group shows and her work was chosen for a national publication of 2009 Best of Artists.

Sharing her talent with others, Margaret has painted as a Barn Artist for several years.

A native of North Carolina, Margaret is also fascinated by genealogy.

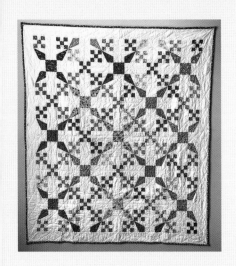

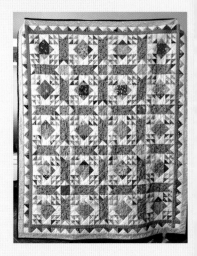

Wendy Skillman

The appliqué quilt "Country Journals" (the chickens) won awards in a few juried shows, which is nice, but it really was a departure from my first love in quilting, which is working in geometrics.

I call myself a quilter because it has always been a constant in my life and I finished my first quilt at age 16. Drawing the design is just as enjoyable for me as making the quilt, and my eye tends to see quilt patterns everywhere. As people were looking up at the Sistine Chapel I was looking down at the incredible mosaic tiles, seeing patterns for quilting!

Hand-sewing gave me something to work on while traveling or sitting in the doctor's office, whereas machine sewing was something I could do at 4:00 in the morning before the kids woke up.

Wherever we lived I would seek out other quilters for feedback on projects, to travel with, laugh, sometimes cry, and just enjoy each other's company, and being with the creative group of Barn Artists has enriched my sense of color and design, and new friendships have been made.

Marilyn Moriarty

After receiving a degree in Fine Arts, Marilyn started teaching art for the next 26 years in her native Rhode Island, as well as in Tequesta, Florida.

She is the busy mother of five, but always found time for her passion, exhibiting her paintings in upscale galleries, which eventually led to countrywide commissions by the Marriott Hotels Group.

Marilyn has founded art groups in Rhode Island and Florida, and she is much loved and appreciated as an active Barn Artist for the past 12 years, where she gladly shares her substantial talent and expertise with others.

We love to laugh with her.

Suzie Goodwin

Suzie Goodwin is a Pennsylvania landscape artist transplanted to Florida about 20 years ago.

"I cannot remember ever not wanting to draw and paint, and I surround myself with like-minded people, learning and sharing."

Suzie has co-founded and joined various art associations and has exhibited her work in Pennsylvania and Florida. Her paintings of personal happenings and their surroundings are of very special meaning to her.

"Pennsylvania and Florida couldn't be more different and I love them both".

Suzie volunteers as an art teacher at Sandy Pines Hospital and Riverbend Academy in Tequesta and is a much valued member of the Barn Artists.

Cindy Cooper

The barn has always been a retreat for me - sometimes solitary, sometimes amongst other artists. Being there is a time to reflect, experiment, expand, grow and to share a love for creativity with others.

The wide open doors, sunlight and the occasional breeze allows for a haven from the busyness of life outside those large, wooden doors.

The barn is a place I cherish.

(Cindy is an established professional artist and the owner of "The Framery" in Hobe Sound. She is known throughout Florida for her excellent work in the restoration of rare paintings.)

Duane Hatfield

Duane owned a business in California, specializing in calligraphy and commercial sign making.

His company was selected to design massive posters for the 1996 Atlanta Olympics.

He now lives in Stuart and does commission paintings, specializing in family dogs.

His whimsical art and his warm personality are loved by everyone, including the Barn Artists.

Lilly Moore

"I have had a passion for art starting at a very young age, and I always appreciate and admire it.

I painted this piece for my college portfolio when I was 16. It is taken out of a triptych of the same boots, the other two done more abstractly.

My teacher instructed me to paint something that is worn and thoroughly used, and these garden boots were the first thing to come to mind. The painting is done in acrylic with gel pen details.

I plan on minoring in art in college so that I can pursue it further, with a major in marketing. Since they go hand in hand, I hope to find a career where I can apply both."

(Lilly is 18 years old and by far the youngest of our gang)

Margot Johnson

Margot's immediate and remaining connection is the joy of Mother Nature. The changing seasons became a part of her life as she explored many areas around her family's Connecticut home.

By sea she delivered sailboats over long distances, which fulfilled her spirit of adventure, and by land she worked in museums in New York City and the Boston Museum of Fine Art.

Margot's watercolor paintings delight the viewer with their bold shapes and brilliant colors.

She has been an active Barn Artist for many years and you can usually find her somewhere in Suzanne's garden, painting from nature with great enthusiasm.

Carol Boye

The emphasis of Carol's work is inspired by the natural beauty of local landscapes she is most familiar with. A long-time resident of Eastern Long Island, she finds her inspiration in the land and seascapes surrounding her waterfront home in Hampton Bays, N.Y.

Carol is an award winning artist and her beautiful oil paintings hang in several galleries in both Florida and New York.

Among her many other talents are dry walling and building houses.

Kathy Forbush

Kathy is an artist from Nahant, Massachusetts, where she lives with a stunning view of the ocean.

Studying under various local instructors she gravitates toward large plein air landscapes and seascapes. A colorist in both oil and watercolor she delights in capturing both light and motion in her work.

Kathy lives in Hobe Sound during the winter and has been a member of the Barn Artists for many years.

Her favorite pastime is baking delicious lemon cupcakes which we all love.

Jeanne Mackin

I hardly consider myself to be an artist, but I will always be an art student.

I was chosen in third grade to take Saturday classes at the Toledo Museum of Art, and that is where my love of art began.

I lived in Saudi Arabia for nine years, modeling for a life drawing class. I was hungry to learn new ways of self-expression in a country where women are not allowed to do so in public, and small, self-directed groups became a creative and intellectual outlet in the home.

When I returned to the a United States, settling in Miami, I suffered from culture shock, missing my international community.

I married Dan Mackin, a famous international artist, who encouraged me to paint again.

Joining the Barn Artists was exactly what I had been craving. I was intimidated at first. So much talent! But it became a wonderful place to paint, learn, share ideas, and real bonds were formed.

Ilse
By Suzanne

Every once on a while a person comes sailing into your life, trailing a bit of magic.

That is Ilse.

When she first appeared in The Barn to paint with the artists, she carried her neat paint box, some special watercolor paper and a happy smile.

The sun was shining and it was a perfect day for catching the light, the breeze and the inspiration to paint something joyful. And joyful her paintings are, depicting colorful birds of all kinds or children playing at the beach, red bucket included.

From the very beginning Ilse was tuned in to her surroundings. She walked around the garden looking at various plants and flowers, and she laughed at the gregarious geckos in my driveway. A small hand shovel would sometimes appear and she would go home with roots, cuttings and seeds, which I love to share, as any gardener does.

I noticed that Ilse sits right down to work, totally concentrating on her art and not making a lot of smalltalk. She sets a good precedent and also gives us ideas, such as painting coconuts and old furniture. She shares her time with others, as we help each other as artists, and she is a valuable asset. Delightful!

We especially love it when she shows up with Belgian chocolate for all of us at lunchtime in the gazebo!

After five years of painting and laughing together, I am delighted to share our paintings, experiences and ideas with you in this book, and we hope you'll enjoy it!

Two different styles.

Hers and mine.

By Ilse

Take Bridge Road to the Beach
By Ilse

It's just a mile or so from the cottage to the beach and sometimes I join Suzanne on one of her bike outings.

The shortest route, straight down Bridge Road, is also the most spectacular: a ride through a tunnel of deep green, created on both sides by grand old Banyan trees so large and stately they hug each other to form a shady, cathedral-like canopy. Depending on the time of day, the intensity of colors vary greatly, ranging from golden in the morning to purple at dusk, inspiring many artists and photographers. Suzanne and I marvel at it every time with fresh appreciation.

The bright, glaring sun at the end of this remarkable tunnel brings us closer to our destination, and I can hear the sound of the ocean waves as if I had my ear pressed to a conch shell.

During the off-season, with hardly a snowbird in sight, we are nearly alone on this long expanse of beach, and the beauty of it makes us go quiet. I never understood, why people feel the need to talk all the time while taking a walk. They totally miss out on nature's grandeur and the inner peace it can bring.

Suzanne and I walk along the water's edge, stooping down now and then to pick up little treasures. We count the pelicans flying above us in a ragged V-formation, we try not to disturb the resting seagulls and we smile at the little flock of Sandpipers fishing for tiny morsels in the retreating waves, then hurrying back to the safety of the sand, their skinny little legs moving so fast, they are a complete blur.

Occasionally we observe Terns or Ospreys, all trying to catch an elusive fish from up high, diving with great speed and courage, often coming up empty, only to try again.

Swimming in the ocean (wave height permitting) gives a feeling of health and well-being, which no spa visit can match. And it's free!

How fortunate to have the ocean so near and so accessible, and we bike back refreshed and surprisingly fulfilled.

I have one regret, however. In the summer I see many wooden stakes high on the beach, placed there by dedicated volunteers, marking the sites of turtle nests. But I have yet to witness the miracle of life: baby turtles hatching and making their urgent scramble to the sea.

How special that would be. Maybe one day.....

A Sample of Suzanne's Artwork

Hassan and the Bees
By Suzanne

Not long after we planted our vegetable garden we decided to distribute six bee boxes throughout the garden, which, once again, had never been sprayed with pesticides.

The bees soon became a garden delight. They thrived among the sweet almond, cherry bushes, mulberries, cocoplums and a variety of other bee-loving plants and flowers.

Hassan became our bee keeper. He installed the large grey wooden boxes and checked them regularly, adding a new queen when needed to keep the hives productive. During the winter he covered the boxes with heavy tarps and old quilts. "Bees do not thrive well in cold weather", he told us.

The honey was delicious, and there was plenty to spare and to share with grateful friends. He used smoke to keep the bees calm in order to remove the honey combs from the boxes.

Hassan was a character. He came from Turkey, where he had a family. He communicated with his wife by phone and pictures. He said that they were happy with that. According to him, the secret to a happy marriage was living in separate countries.

Hassan loved to smoke the bee boxes, and with great success. But sometimes, sporting a mischievous grin, he would reach in too fast and enjoy watching the bees becoming angry, swarming all over the place and chasing the artists out of the barn. He always seemed to arrive on the day when we artists met in the barn to paint!

One morning, Hassan arrived to open the beehive in the front garden behind the picket fence. For some odd reason he decided to skip his usual smoke method and, dislodged from their home, the bees became angry and started to attack whoever was near. Hassan lost control, grabbing the garden hose.

By that time, neighbors and others became alarmed, running for cover. The bees were swarming! Some inventive soul cranked up a citronella sprayer and the surrounding area, sidewalk and street, were lost in a mist of white fog.

Hassan was nowhere to be seen. I decided to leave for the beach. The whole neighborhood was in an uproar!

It was reported to me later that someone called the police and a deputy appeared. Unfortunately, the bees went straight for him as well, as he tried to figure out how to restore order in the neighborhood. He was seen running across the park to the community center, gun jiggling behind and bees in hot pursuit.

I decided to stay away for the rest of the day. When I finally returned, the coast was clear and Hassan was gone. He had driven his old grey van, including a few angry left-over bees, to the other side of town. He was wearing an empty water cooler container over his head for protection.

The last we heard was that a frightened resident in that neighborhood had seen Hassan in his strange getup and had called the county to inquire about possible aliens from space in the area!

So much for bees!

HASSAN AND THE BEE BOXES

A PLATE OF YUMMY HONEY

Churches
By Suzanne

We are fortunate to live between two churches.

THE HOBE SOUND COMMUNITY CHURCH is Presbyterian. Sometime in the 1930s the prominent Reed family from Jupiter Island donated land for the construction of the church. It was simple but well attended, and the grateful congregation grew over the years. Later, during the 1960s, a splendid ceiling was added. It consisted of hand painted biblical flowers in beautiful colors and they delight worshippers to this day.

The church's tall white steeple reaches high above the trees and into a wide blue sky, and its tin roof gleams in the sunshine. A large brick yard dotted with beautiful flowering vines invites parishioners and friends to mingle and enjoy life. During the winter months, front doors swing wide open and music and singing can be heard from the street.

With its old wood Florida shutters and peaceful sanctuary the church is a rare gift for our community as a substantial part of our history and as a center for us all.

ST. CHRISTOPHER is a Catholic Church along U.S. Highway 1. It has a stunning gold dome and its lovely bells ring out over the neighborhood.

The ground on which it is built was once the home of Jobe Indians for thousands of years, before folks like us arrived.

The land for the construction of the church was donated, and as the congregation grew, so did the buildings, expanding to add a graceful Italianate courtyard with a beautifully landscaped garden, a perfect place for solitude and prayer.

The congregation is led by an Irish priest. During the winter months the church offers concerts, Irish comedy evenings, and a powerful operatic tenor often leads in song. The church's colorful modern stained glass windows add a glorious scene of originality and beauty. The designs for these rare windows came from Spain.

Father Cann, a past priest at the church, once told me that his dad had been the manager of the first Coca-Cola bottling plant in Miami, a unique and important position at the time. Father Cann was responsible for the designing and installation of the stained glass windows. He ordered a piece of a Coca-Cola bottle to be included in the glass, its exact location a secret. Look for it! You may find it somewhere in one of the windows.

St. Christopher's windows,
where history and nature blend
in harmony.

Places of the Past
By Suzanne

After I moved into Osprey Cottage, I began to paint my surroundings, paying special attention to our historical buildings, which I felt were in need of well-deserved recognition.

Most of them date from 1900 to the 1940s. Some of them have changed hands and names since then, some no longer exist.

I am glad that I accepted the commissions to paint them at the time, so that they can have a place in our memory and in this book.

Take a walk through a few pages of painted local history.

Village Feed
Once serving the farming community, torn down

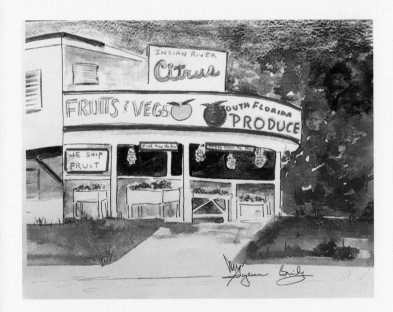

Indian River Citrus
Reported to have once been used for alligator
wrestling in the 1920s

Pettway Food Shop
An old and familiar place along the railroad tracks serving the
surrounding neighborhood

Algozzini
Colorful Hawaiian marketplace selling shells, tropical
shirts, gifts and souvenirs

Community Center
Moved from Camp Murphy, in what is now Johnathan Dickinson State Park, at the end of World War II, where it was used as barracks for the soldiers.

Harry and the Natives
In the 1930s and 40s the site had cabins and gas pumps. The restaurant was built of tidewater pecky cypress from a creek on the Loxahatchee River, and the Grand Opening was on Pearl Harbor Day, 1941.
A true landmark to this day.

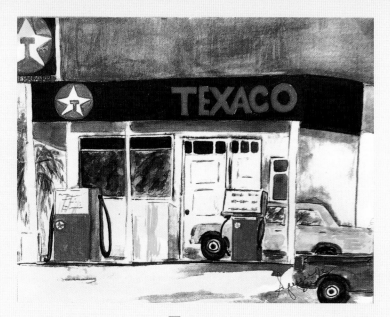

Texaco
Formerly known as 'Diamond's Garage', a gas station
from years past, belonged to an original
Hobe Sound family

Apollo School
Built in 1925 as a two-room school house in what was
then called the town of 'Olympia', neglected since 1963,
restored, and today houses the local historical museum.

Hobe Sound Railroad Station
Welcomed people to a sparsely populated area 100 years ago. As passenger trains were discontinued years later, the building was moved to a place nearby and is awaiting its future fate.

The Hair Company
Buildings that once were barracks, canteens and wash houses were transplanted from the former Camp Murphy army base throughout Hobe Sound, including The Hair Company.

Murder at the Mermaid Bar

By Suzanne

An Oldtimer told me about the Mermaid Bar. The story goes:

Once upon a time there was a lively bar in Hobe Sound, frequented by soldiers stationed at Camp Murphy during WW2 in what is now Jonathan Dickinson State Park. In the middle of the room a parquet dance floor, polished and shining, stood ready for Saturday night's dancing. The smoky bar was regularly filled with service men eager for a good time. Dancing, laughing, flirting with local girls, and plenty of drinking. The place was rocking.

One particular night there was a nasty scene, when a jealous husband found his wife in the arms of her lover, dancing much too amorously in front of everyone. They had been doing more than dancing! There was much shouting and shoving and name calling, when all of a sudden the enraged husband pulled out a pistol and ended the evening with a loud, ear-splitting shot, eliminating his rival.

A murder! How horribly exciting! Just like in the movies!

The old building of Mermaid fame, now a landscape and garden center, is still standing next to the fire station on US Highway 1, unnoticed by speeding cars. The story lives on, embellished over time. The old dance floor, however, didn't improve with age. It is still there, forgotten, covered with a large, raggedy old oriental rug, and if you lift a corner of it, you can make out the parquet pattern, grey, rotten and buckling.

The mermaid is gone.

In my imagination, though, I can still hear the stomping, the music, the laughter.

Ilse

An Oink and a Bark in Zeus Park
By Suzanne

There is no doubt that dogs make life richer and happier. They fit right into the lifestyle of cottage living, with so many treasures to topple or to investigate. They love lying in front of a wood fire in the winter and playing in the garden in the summertime, chasing frogs, rabbits and other hidden creatures.

In our neighborhood we celebrate "Yappy Hour", with dogs and their owners getting together under the spreading oak trees in a large green park, to have fun yacking and yapping at one another.

Often Greta, the pig, shows up with her owner and joins the fun. She has a spiffing good time, tail rotating in helicopter fashion while snorting around in the grass. Several dogs think she is one of their kind and have romantic ideas, while others hope she will give them attention and play.

Rotund Greta is solid black, has long eyelashes and weighs about 13 lbs. Squealing with delight when held, she is undoubtedly queen of the day. Running along behind others, tail whirling and ears flying, she does not want to be left behind. Often, all tuckered out, she falls asleep for brief periods of time, standing up straight! Greta is quite smart and also can swim, her proud owner tells us.

"Yappy Hour" is delightful when Greta comes to play.

Ilse

Suzanne

"IT'S NEVER TOO LATE TO

HAVE A HAPPY CHILDHOOD"

Ed Briley

CHEERS!

Here's to all the people who live life to the fullest.

Dedication

This book is a labor of love. Love for nature, art, music, and for the people who have encouraged us to write and illustrate it.

A special Thank You goes to our dear friend James D. Snyder, himself a distinguished author of eight books. Jim's imaginative suggestions added spice and humor to our musings and we will always be in his debt.

He was paid with home-baked chocolate chip cookies.